This book
belongs to:

....

R is for Reindeer

A *is for*

Angel

I spy with my little eye somthing starting with

O is for

Ornament

S is for
Snowman

G is for

Gift

B *is for*

Bell

D *is for*

Decoration

W *is for*

Wreath

I spy with my little eye somthing starting with

I spy with my little eye somthing starting with

P is for

Pie

C is for

Candle

I spy with my little eye somthing starting with

F is for

Firewood

I spy And count:

 _____

 _____

 _____

 _____

I spied

  6

 5

 8

 9

I spy And count:

 _____

 _____

 _____

I spied

  10    6

  7    6

I spy And count:

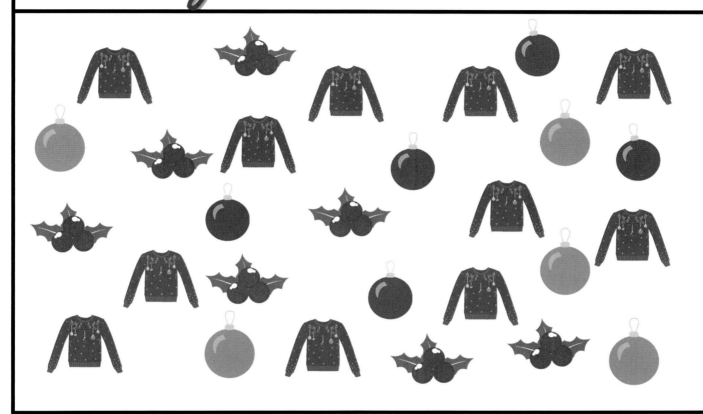

I spied

 5

 11

 7

 5

I spy And count:

 _____

 _____

I spied

 8

 6

 5

 5